Discover bugs with photos, fun facts, and verse

BUGS

Exploring the World of Crawly Critters

Written by Dr. Shirley Raines

Photography by Curt Hart

Integrating science and art creates a valuable and unique learning experience that particularly benefits the youngest of readers. STEAM (science, technology, engineering, art, and mathematics) education inspires a wider audience to invest in studying subjects from multiple perspectives and promotes an education that suits many types of learners.

In this introduction to bugs and their unique features, artistic and scientific elements are combined to create a comprehensive learning experience for young readers.

Continue the learning with a selection of engaging exercises in the back of the book. These Story S-t-r-e-t-c-h-e-r-s by Dr. Shirley Raines expand the material with a variety of activities perfect for learning both in and out of the classroom.

A glossary can also be found in the back of the book with words and definitions that help build upon the vocabulary from both the poetry and facts.

Music to My Ears:
The Life of a Cricket

Crickets are known for their musical chirping. Male crickets are the only ones who can chirp. They have special organs located on their wings that they rub together to create the sound.

Male crickets chirp to attract a mate or to fend off a potential rival.

In China, crickets are a symbol of good luck and were even kept as pets by the nobility in the Imperial era.

Crickets have large antennae. A cricket's antennae can often be longer than their entire body.

A group of crickets is called an orchestra.

Crickets can be brown, black, green, or sometimes even red.

Ladybug Luck

Ladybug, land on me
so I can count your spots.
Seven, five, or three?
How many dots?

Ladybug with tiny wings
and hard outer shell.
Quiet, no song to sing.
Beetle or bug, who can tell?

Red with shell so hard.
Lucky ladybug, do not flee.
Eating aphids in my yard.
Ladybug, land on me.

Can You Spot the Ladybug?

When a ladybug is in its pupal stage, it doesn't actually have its famous dots. The dots on ladybugs don't appear until they become adults. Even then, it can take hours or days for the spots to appear as the ladybug grows its shell.

A ladybug's distinct red or orange coloring tells predators not to eat them.

Ladybugs are sometimes called ladybirds.

NASA once sent a few ladybugs into space to see how aphids would escape from the ladybugs in zero gravity.

Dragonfly Beauty

Dragonflies are such beautiful things
with four lovely translucent wings.

Dragonfly hovering in the sky,
sideways and backwards you fly.

Capture your prey in mid-air;
food caught anywhere.

Dragonfly may sound a little scary,
but there is no need to be wary.

Taking Flight

Dragonflies are known for their impressive ability to fly. Dragonflies can fly in any direction and even change direction on the stop of a dime. They use these super flying powers to help them catch their food, which typically consists of flies and mosquitoes.

Large dragonflies can fly as fast as 35 miles per hour (56.3 kilometers per hour).

A dragonfly's eyes are so big they almost cover its entire head.

Dragonflies spend most of their life underwater as nymphs. Even as adults, dragonflies typically like to live near water.

Creepy, Crawly Cockroaches

Creepy, crawly cockroaches come through cracks in the wall.
Turn on the light and see them scurry down the hall.
Dropped some crumbs from my sweet cake.
Mom said, "That is all it will take!"

Tidy up the kitchen and sweep it clean.
Do not leave a single thing!

Small cockroaches can grow large
if we do not take charge.
Mind the food left behind.
Don't leave food of any kind!

Not So Picky Eaters

Cockroaches eat just about anything. They seem to enjoy many of the foods we like to eat, such as meat, sugary foods, and bread. They are also known to feast on hair, glue, paper, old clothes, and leather. Some even eat wood. Cockroaches can live for months without food as long as they have water.

Cockroaches are nocturnal. The 2,000 lenses in their compound eyes help them navigate in the dark.

Cockroaches can hold their breath for 40 minutes underwater.

Cockroaches have existed for more than 350 million years, making them older than some dinosaurs!

Hop to It, Grasshopper!

Grasshoppers are known for their excellent ability to jump. They stretch their back legs and extend them forward with great force.

Grasshoppers jump to escape a predator. A grasshopper can leap up to 20 times the length of its body.

Grasshoppers eat flowers, weeds, corn, and grass.

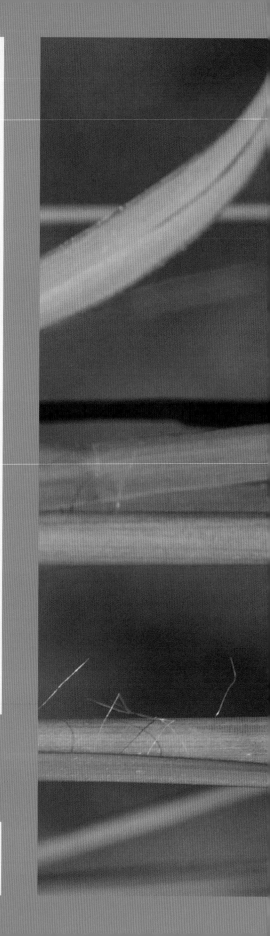

Grasshoppers don't have ears, but they are able to detect sound from an organ on their abdomen, right below their wings.

Grasshoppers have two wings, meaning they are able to fly.

A grasshopper has five eyes. Two compound eyes on either side of its head and three simple eyes on the front of its head.

Damselflies on Lily Pads

I saw a damselfly on a lily pad today.
It landed for a second then flew away.

These graceful damsels with their big eyes
are such a lovely afternoon surprise.

They float and flit and fly around
in colors olive green or brown.

Their wings all glitter, flash, and show,
attracting the attention of fish below.

I saw a damselfly on a lily pad today.
I sure wish it was here to stay.

Damsel NOT in Distress

They may have damsel in their name, but damselflies are actually considered predators. They eat flies, mosquitoes, moths, and even caterpillars. They can eat hundreds of thousands of insects in a single summer. Much like its cousin the dragonfly, a damselfly's flying ability and large compound eyes help it see and catch its prey.

When resting, damselflies hold their wings above their backs while dragonflies hold their wings out like an airplane.

Much like dragonflies, damselflies cannot walk using their legs even though they have six of them.

The biggest species of damselfly is the helicopter damselfly. It has a wingspan of 7.5 inches (19.1 centimeters).

Off My Flowers, Japanese Beetle!

Snipping flowers from my yard,
saw an insect with back so hard.
Crawling on a very small leaf,
eating my flowers. Good grief!

Are more Japanese beetles around?
On another petal, there I found
more beetles eating in full sunlight,
nibbling on pretty leaves with delight.

I hoped they would fly
to the poison ivy plants nearby.
It would make such a tasty treat
for these small beetles to eat.

These half-inch beetles in length
have such extraordinary strength.
Can bring this gardener to her knees.
Leave my garden, pretty please!

Bad to the Bone

Japanese beetles are originally from Japan. Since their arrival, these beetles have developed a bad reputation for eating crops, plants, and flowers. The way Japanese beetles eat plants is called skeletonization. After they eat the leafy parts of a plant, the remaining parts look like lace.

The lifespan of an adult Japanese beetle is only a little over a month.

If you look closely, you can see a row of white furry spots on either side of an adult Japanese beetle.

Japanese beetles love the sunshine. You are most likely to spot one on a warm, sunny day.

Pee-yew! What Stinks?

Stink bugs stink! A stink bug begins to stink when it releases a smelly liquid from the holes in its abdomen when it's either scared, being attacked, or nervous.

The stinky odor tells predators to leave them alone. The odor also tells other stink bugs where to find them.

The brown marmorated stink bug can be found in about 40 of the 50 states in the US and up to five provinces in Canada.

Their needle-shaped mouth is used to poke through fruit and plants in order to suck out the juices.

Stink bugs breathe through tiny holes in their stomach.

In the winter, stink bugs will search for a warm place to enter diapause, a form of hibernation.

Walking Stick Disguises

A walking stick is an insect,
avoiding a bird's sharp peck.
Hidden in plain sight
with no wings for flight.

Latched onto a leaf or stem,
looking like a wooden limb.
Colored in green, gray, or brown,
seldom found on the ground.

Some are long—over a foot!
But on a limb, they stay put.
Others less than an inch
have bodies that do not twitch.

Staying still as still can be,
the walking stick you may not see.
Standing still in its frozen pose,
hiding right in front of your nose.

Masters of Disguise

Walking stick bugs are known for being experts in camouflage, which allows them to blend into their environments and hide from potential predators. In order to convince predators that they are indeed just sticks or leaves, walking stick bugs will stay very still or even sway like a branch in the wind.

Some species can detach their legs to escape a predator. Their missing leg then grows back later!

Some species of walking stick bugs can slowly change the color of their body to hide from predators.

The longest walking stick bug in the world is about 2 feet (61 centimeters) long.

Praying Mantis, Do You Pray?

With strong forelegs poised near its face,
praying mantis seems to say grace.
Praying for food, it may seem,
waiting on a flower serene.

When praying mantises are small,
aphids are great to eat overall.
As they grow, larger insects are their treat,
catching flies, grasshoppers, and moths to eat.

Heads with large eyes that move easily,
waiting and watching for prey patiently.
With strong forelegs together clasped,
its surprised prey is quickly grasped.

PREYing Mantis

Praying mantises get their name from their very unique front legs. These special limbs are folded as if the mantis is praying when it is waiting for its meal. As soon as its prey comes within reach, the praying mantis will quickly extend its front legs and grab it. These front legs aren't only quick, they have spikes to ensure its prey doesn't get away while it eats!

A praying mantis can turn its head 180 degrees.

Some praying mantises have wings and are able to fly.

Female praying mantises bite or even eat potential mates!

Shoo, Fly. Don't Bother Me!

One of the most amazing facts about houseflies is their ability to stick to objects and walls.

They have sticky adhesive pads known as pulvilli. Flies even have claws to unstick themselves from surfaces so they can fly away.

Houseflies don't have mouths to eat solid foods. They mainly consume liquids.

Flies have taste receptors on their feet which is why they make so many landings. They are tasting a potential meal.

Flies carry germs on their feet. These germs cause diseases.

Female houseflies are larger than males and have more space between their eyes.

Blink and Glow Little Firefly

· ·

In summer, the firefly flies,
eluding chasers in the skies.

Their twinkles make such a sight,
blinking on and off at night.

Yellow, green, or amber blink,
keeping their flashing all in sync.

When I chase fireflies in my yard,
I try to catch them in a jar.

Caught a firefly. It flashed its light.
Such a pretty, wondrous sight!

Open the jar and let it go.
I watch it fly then blink and glow.

Let There Be Light

Fireflies glow due to something called bioluminescence. A chemical reaction happens in an organ on the firefly's abdomen which is why they light up. The light that is produced can be yellow, pale red, or green. Most fireflies are nocturnal. Some fireflies are out during the day, but they typically are a type that doesn't produce light.

Fireflies produce cold light which means it doesn't give off any heat.

Fireflies aren't actually flies. They are part of the beetle family.

If a firefly feels threatened, it will release drops of blood that contain bitter tasting chemicals.

Katydid, Katydid, Katydid Search

Hear a cricket? Is that the sound?
But no cricket could be found.
"Katydid, katydid, katydid?"

At dusk in a woodsy green glen,
looking for insects again.
"Katydid, katydid, katydid?"

I heard the katydid chorus.
Louder, the noise moved toward us.
"Katydid, katydid, katydid?"

Just green insects on green leaves,
stealing night silence like thieves.
"Katydid, katydid, katydid?"

Insects rubbing on forewings.
Always such noisy things!
"Katydid, katydid, katydid?"

Hiding in plain sight,
making noises that fill the night.
"Katydid, katydid, katydid?"

Katydid, Cricket, or Grasshopper?

Listening to the katydid, it could be easy to confuse it for a cricket. In England and Ireland, they are often called bush crickets. Some people call them long-horned grasshoppers. You can tell them apart from grasshoppers because katydids have longer and narrower antennae.

Many species of katydid live in the Amazon rainforest, but there are over 250 species in North America alone.

Katydids are great at disguises. They can make themselves look just like leaves.

Katydids are most often heard at the end of the summer.

STORY S-T-R-E-T-C-H-E-R-S

Stretch out the learning with this collection of activities created specifically to enhance the material and provide new ways to discover the wonderful world of bugs. From language arts to science, each activity incorporates information from the book and provides a new approach to teaching early learners in and out of the classroom. For more Story S-t-r-e-t-c-h-e-r-s, please visit www.FlowerpotPress.com.

Story S-t-r-e-t-c-h-e-r for ART

What the children will learn
To identify and make translucent and luminescent representations of dragonflies

Materials
Wax paper, luminescent crayons, pencils, construction paper, scissors, glue, plastic fishing wire (optional), and colorful plastic sheets (optional)

What to do
1. Show children photographs of various dragonflies. Highlight each of their characteristics. Emphasize the terms translucent and luminescent especially when referring to their wings.
2. Distribute wax paper. Let children use luminescent crayons to draw patterns on the wax paper, being careful to leave the wax paper colorful but still translucent.
3. Have children draw a dragonfly body without the wings on construction paper. Use some of the luminescent crayons to decorate the head and body of the dragonfly.
4. Carefully cut out the dragonfly bodies.
5. Glue the dragonfly bodies onto the decorated wax paper.
6. Draw the outlines of wings around the dragonfly bodies on the wax paper.
7. Carefully cut out the bodies and wings of the dragonflies.

Something to think about
Consider displaying the dragonflies by hanging them from the ceiling with plastic fishing wire. Older children might use various colors of plastic sheets to create their dragonfly wings.

Story S-t-r-e-t-c-h-e-r for SCIENCE

What the children will learn
To study one insect in-depth and report on their findings

Materials
The book, paper, large index cards, rulers, pencils, and various art supplies

What to do
1. Learn about a K-W-L chart. K means what we already know about the bug we selected. W means what we want to know. L means what we have learned.
2. Model the K-W-L process with a bug of particular interest to you.
3. Ask each child to select one of the bugs described in the book. Encourage partners or teams of bug experts if more than one child wants to study the same bug.
4. Let the children have several days to research their bugs from the book and write their K-W-L charts.
5. Have a Bug Expert Day for children to share what they have learned with the class.

Something to think about
Encourage children to make different models of their bugs from clay, playdough, or computer illustrations to use when they are the presenter.

Story S-t-r-e-t-c-h-e-r for LANGUAGE ARTS

What the children will learn
To identify and use rhyming words in poetry and create their own poems with what they have learned

Materials
The book, chart tablet or whiteboard, and markers

What to do
1. Print the "Dragonfly Beauty" poem on the chart tablet or whiteboard.
2. Omit the final word from the second line of each stanza.
3. Read the poem to the children and let them supply the rhyming words from the second line. For example, "wings" rhymes with "things."
4. Complete the poem, filling in the rhyming words.
5. Read the "Ladybug Luck" poem aloud. Help the children to identify the rhyming words and make a list. For example, "three" rhymes with "me," "wings" rhymes with "sing," and "hard" rhymes with "yard."
6. Have children come up with new rhyming words for the second line of each stanza to create a brand new poem.

Something to think about
Let children choose a poem or a part of a poem to memorize. The rhyming words make the poems more memorable. Have children determine the meaning of words they do not usually read by the context of the poem or other information found about the bug. Encourage more advanced students to write their own bug poems.

GLOSSARY

Abdomen: the back part of the body on an insect

Antennae: rod-shaped body parts found on an insect's head; used to smell and maintain balance

Aphids: a tiny bug ladybugs like to eat

Bioluminescence: when an animal is able to produce light

Camouflage: the coloration or ability of an animal to appear like its surroundings

Forelegs: the two front legs on an animal or insect

Hibernation: when an animal hides away for the winter in a warm location

Insect: a type of animal with six legs, a thorax, a head, an abdomen, an exoskeleton, two antennae, and compound eyes

Lifespan: how long an animal lives

Pulvilli: pads on the claws of flies that allow them to stick to surfaces

Pupal: the life stage between larva and adult

Skeletonization: removing the leafy parts of a plant which can stop it from growing

Species: a group of animals with similar characteristics

Compound Eye: a type of eye certain bugs have which is made up of thousands of lenses

Diapause: when an insect lowers its body temperature and activity level during a very cold or very warm time of year

Nocturnal: mostly active at night

Predator: an animal that hunts other animals in order to get food

Prey: an animal that is hunted by other animals